44 Fast and Effective Solutions to Diarrhea and Stomach Aches:

44 Meal Recipes to Help You Recover in No Time

By

Joe Correa CSN

COPYRIGHT

© 2016 Live Stronger Faster Inc.

All rights reserved

Reproduction or translation of any part of this work beyond that permitted by section 107 or 108 of the 1976 United States Copyright Act without the permission of the copyright owner is unlawful.

This publication is designed to provide accurate and authoritative information in regard to the subject matter covered. It is sold with the understanding that neither the author nor the publisher is engaged in rendering medical advice. If medical advice or assistance is needed, consult with a doctor. This book is considered a guide and should not be used in any way detrimental to your health. Consult with a physician before starting this nutritional plan to make sure it's right for you.

ACKNOWLEDGEMENTS

This book is dedicated to my friends and family that have had mild or serious illnesses so that you may find a solution and make the necessary changes in your life.

44 Fast and Effective Solutions to Diarrhea and Stomach Aches:

44 Meal Recipes to Help You Recover in No Time

By

Joe Correa CSN

CONTENTS

Copyright

Acknowledgements

About The Author

Introduction

44 Fast and Effective Solutions to Diarrhea and Stomach Aches: 44 Meal Recipes to Help You Recover in No Time

Additional Titles from This Author

ABOUT THE AUTHOR

After years of Research, I honestly believe in the positive effects that proper nutrition can have over the body and mind. My knowledge and experience has helped me live healthier throughout the years and which I have shared with family and friends. The more you know about eating and drinking healthier, the sooner you will want to change your life and eating habits.

Nutrition is a key part in the process of being healthy and living longer so get started today. The first step is the most important and the most significant.

INTRODUCTION

Diarrhea and stomach cramps are bacterial or viral infections usually caused by food or low-quality water. However, frequent or constant problems can be serious medical conditions that should be treated at a hospital. These medical problems require a balanced diet rich in fiber and good carbs, probiotics, balanced proteins, and healthy fats. In other words, your body needs to get rid of the toxins in your stomach and the best way is always the natural way, through food.

Our gastrointestinal system is a complex ecosystem that needs to be provided with the proper nutrients to maintain optimal health. This book will provide you with recipes that will do just that.

Intestinal microflora has an important role in:

- ✓ creating a powerful immune system
- ✓ developing a normal intestinal morphology
- ✓ maintaining chronic immune-mediated inflammatory response
- ✓ maintaining the function of intestinal mucosal defense against allergens
- ✓ helping to prevent the attachment of pathogenic microorganisms

About 40% of the population have some sort of problem with their gastrointestinal tract. These are "the big four" – the most common symptoms when something is out of balance:

1. abdominal pain
2. diarrhea
3. indigestion
4. heartburn

However, these symptoms can be easily treated with these simple lifestyle changes: reorganize your diet and avoid stress. A lot of pharmacy remedies can help with short-term relief, but you have to keep in mind that only a major lifestyle change will actually solve the problem.

These stomach friendly recipes are based on healthy ingredients and are carefully designed to help you follow your new regime. You will find plenty of effective recipes for breakfast, lunch, dinner, salads, and snacks.

44 FAST AND EFFECTIVE SOLUTIONS TO DIARRHEA AND STOMACH ACHES: 44 MEAL RECIPES TO HELP YOU RECOVER IN NO TIME

Breakfast Recipes

1. Eggs with Tomato and Spring Onions

Ingredients:

3 whole eggs

1 medium-sized tomato, sliced

3 spring onions, chopped

¼ tsp of salt

¼ tsp of cayenne pepper

2 tbsp of butter

Preparation:

Melt the butter in a frying skillet over a medium-high temperature. Add onions and stir-fry for 2 minutes.

Now add tomato slices, salt and cayenne pepper. Stir-fry tomato slices for about a minute one each side.

Meanwhile, beat the eggs and add to a frying skillet. Cook for about 30 seconds.

Nutrition information per serving: Kcal: 257, Protein: 19g, Carbs: 5g, Fats: 17g

2. No-Bake Protein Balls with Oats

Ingredients:

1 ½ cup of rolled oats plus

½ cup of peanut butter

¼ cup of minced almonds

3 tablespoons of honey

1 tablespoon of minced chia seeds

1 tbsp of vanilla extract

3 cups of milk

Preparation:

Place one cup of rolled oats in a bowl. Add other dry ingredients and stir to combine.

Now add in peanut butter and honey. Mix well and gently pour in the milk and vanilla extract. Shape the balls using your hands, top with the remaining oats and place in the refrigerator for about 30 minutes.

Nutrition information per serving: Kcal: 425, Protein: 31g, Carbs: 48g, Fats: 10.5g

3. Chocolate Balls

Ingredients:

1 cup of minced almonds

½ cup of peanut butter

½ cup of honey

2 tablespoons of minced chia seeds

¼ cup of raw cocoa powder

¼ cup of grated dark chocolate

¼ cup of milk

Preparation:

Combine the ingredients in a bowl and mix well to combine. Shape the balls using your hands and refrigerate for about 30 minutes.

Nutrition information per serving: Kcal: 430, Protein: 27g, Carbs: 50g, Fats: 11g

4. Spinach Omelet

Ingredients:

3 eggs, whole and beaten

½ cup cottage cheese

½ cup of onion, peeled and chopped

1 cup of fresh spinach, finely chopped

1 tbsp of olive oil

salt and pepper, to taste

Preparation:

Heat up the olive oil over a medium temperature. Stir-fry the onions until translucent.

Crack the eggs and mix well with a fork. Add some salt and pepper. Whisk in 1 cup of fresh spinach and ½ cup of cottage cheese. Pour the eggs evenly in a pan and reduce the heat. Cook for about 2 minutes, stirring constantly.

Nutrition information per serving: Kcal: 470, Protein: 32g, Carbs: 9.5g, Fats: 21g

5. Homemade Fig Spread

Ingredients:

1 pound dry figs, cut into small pieces

6 tbsp powdered stevia

2 tbsp fresh lemon juice

1 cup milk

Preparation:

In a small saucepan, combine the figs, stevia, and fresh lemon juice. Add 1/2 cup of milk and bring it to a boil.

Reduce the heat to low and add the remaining milk. Depending on your taste, you can add some more milk. Cook for about 20 minutes. When done, transfer to a food processor and blend until smooth mixture.

Nutrition information per serving: Kcal: 300, Protein: 5g, Carbs: 66g, Fats: 1g

6. Pumpkin Seeds Oatmeal

Ingredients:

1 cup of rolled oats

1 tbsp of pumpkin seeds

2 cups of skim milk

½ cup of water

2 egg whites

½ cup of maple syrup

1 tsp of cinnamon, ground

Preparation:

Preheat the oven to 350 degrees. Spread the pumpkin seeds on a baking sheet and toast for about 5-6 minutes. You want a nice lightly brown color.

Boil the 2 cups of skim milk and ½ cup of water over a high temperature. Add the oats, egg whites and stir well. Cook for another 7 minutes, or until the oats are cooked. Stir in the pumpkin seeds. Remove from the heat and let it stand for 10 minutes. Serve with some cinnamon on top.

Nutrition information per serving: Kcal: 168, Protein: 5.1g, Carbs: 30g, Fats: 1.9g

7. Wild Berries Muesli

Ingredients:

1 cup rolled oats

¼ cup fresh apple juice

½ cup wild berries

2 tbsp honey

1 cup milk

Preparation:

Place the oats in a large bowl. Add fresh apple juice and milk. Cover and let it stand in the refrigerator for about an hour.

Add honey and stir well. Top with wild berries and serve.

Nutrition information per serving: Kcal: 281, Protein: 10g, Carbs: 48g, Fats: 4g

8. Breakfast Tuna Spread

Ingredients:

1 medium-sized tuna fillet

1 small onion, peeled

3 tbsp olive oil

¼ tsp black pepper

¼ tsp sea salt

1 tsp dry rosemary

Preparation:

Wash and pat dry the fillet. Cut into bite size pieces and set aside.

Heat up the oil in a large skillet and add the tuna chops. Cook for about ten minutes stirring constantly. Remove from the heat.

Meanwhile, combine the ingredients in a blender. Add tuna and mix well for about 30 seconds. Enjoy!

Nutrition information per serving: Kcal: 275, Protein: 26g, Carbs: 0g, Fats: 19g

9. Grilled Eggplant Slices

Ingredients:

1 large eggplant

3 eggs

¼ tsp of sea salt

1 tbsp of olive oil

½ tsp of cinnamon

Preparation:

Peel eggplant and cut into slices. Sprinkle some salt on each side of eggplant. Allow it to rest for about 15 minutes. Meanwhile, mix eggs with cinnamon in a large bowl. Heat up the olive oil in frying pan over a medium temperature.

Put the eggplant slices in the egg mixture. Make few holes with a knife to allow the mixture to permeate the eggplant. Fry it until golden brown color, on each side. This should take about 10 minutes. Serve your eggplant slices warm.

Nutrition information per serving: Kcal: 65, Protein: 3.8g, Carbs: 9g, Fats: 3.6g

10. Scrambled Eggs with Turmeric

Ingredients:

2 eggs

1 egg white

1 tbsp of olive oil

1 tsp of ground turmeric

salt and pepper to taste

Preparation:

Grease the frying pan with olive oil. Heat up over to medium-high heat. Meanwhile, whisk together eggs, egg white and turmeric. Add some salt and pepper to taste and fry for few minutes.

Nutrition information per serving: Kcal: 71, Protein: 21g, Carbs: 2g, Fats: 8g

Lunch Recipes

11. Tortellini with Cheese Sauce

Ingredients:

1 (16 ounces) package frozen cheese tortellini (choose rice flour, vegan tortellini)

3 cups of vegetable broth

1 cup of cashew cream

2 tbsp of whipped cooking cream, dairy-free

2oz tofu, grated

¼ tsp of cayenne pepper

A handful of fresh parsley, finely chopped

Preparation:

In a deep pot, bring 3 cups of vegetable broth to boil. Add frozen cheese tortellini and cook for 3-4 minutes. (The cooking time depends on your tortellini. Use package instructions). Remove from the heat and drain.

Reduce the heat to minimum and add the grated tofu. Slowly pour in the cashew cream, whipped cooking cream and cayenne pepper. Cook for a couple of minutes.

Transfer the tortellini to a plate, top with cheese sauce and sprinkle with chopped parsley.

Serve warm.

Nutrition information per 1 serving: Kcal: 521 Protein: 28g, Carbs: 56.4g, Fats: 13g

12. Pressure Cooker's Beans

Ingredients:

1 ½ pound of beans, pre - cooked

2 medium – sized carrots, sliced

1 large red pepper, chopped

2 medium – sized onions, sliced

5 gloves of garlic, minced

3 small – sized tomatoes, sliced

1 cup of tomato sauce

1 small chili pepper

1 cup of sliced celery

2 tbsp of olive oil

7 glasses of water

Preparation:

With the cooker's lid off, heat the olive oil on high. Stir-fry the onions for 2 minutes.

Add sliced carrots, pepper and garlic. Cook for about 10 minutes on high temperature. Then add the tomatoes, tomato sauce, and 1 more glass of hot water.

Add the pre-cooked beans and 5 glasses of water. Now add the celery and chili pepper.

Securely lock the cooker's lid. Set for 10 minutes on high.

Nutrition information per 1 serving: Kcal: 356 Protein: 9g, Carbs: 49g, Fats: 6g

13. Roasted Chicken

Ingredients:

1 whole chicken

1 tsp salt

Preparation:

Wash and clean the chicken. Evenly sprinkle the salt all over chicken.

Preheat the oven to 350 degrees F. Place the chicken in a baking sheet, over a baking paper.

Roast for about an hour.

Nutrition information per 1 serving: Kcal: 371 Protein: 38g, Carbs: 0g, Fats: 16g

14. Moroccan Rice

Ingredients:

1 cup of brown rice

2 tbsp. extra virgin olive oil

2 medium-sized carrots, grated

1 small tomato, peeled and finely chopped

1 tbsp. Moroccan spice seasoning

1 medium-sized onion, peeled and chopped

6-7 dried apricots, halved

Preparation:

In a deep pot, bring 3 cups of water to a boiling point. Add rice, reduce the heat to minimum, and cook until the water evaporates. Remove from the heat.

Heat up the olive oil in a frying pan. Add onion and stir-fry until translucent. Now add tomato, apricots, and Moroccan spice seasoning. Cook for five more minutes and add rice. Stir well to combine.

Top with grated carrots and serve.

Nutrition information per 1 serving: Kcal: 435 Protein: 15.9g, Carbs: 67g, Fats: 6.3g

15. Broccoli Stew

Ingredients:

2oz fresh broccoli

A handful of fresh parsley, finely chopped

1 tsp of dry thyme

1 tbsp of fresh lemon juice

¼ tsp of ground chili pepper

3 tbsp of olive oil

1 tbsp of cashew cream

Preparation:

Place the broccoli in a deep pot and pour enough water to cover. Bring it to a boil and cook until tender. Remove from the heat and drain.

Transfer to a food processor. Add fresh parsley, thyme, and about ½ cup of water. Pulse until smooth mixture. Return to a pot and add some more water. Bring it to a boil and cook for several minutes, over a minimum temperature.

Stir in some olive oil and cashew cream, sprinkle with ground chili pepper and add fresh lemon juice. Serve warm.

Nutrition information per 1 serving: Kcal: 72 Protein: 12g, Carbs: 15.8g, Fats: 8g

16. Light Mac and Tuna

Ingredients:

1 cup of minced tuna

½ cup of homemade cashew cream

2 cups of rice flour macaroni

1 tsp of sea salt

1 tsp of olive oil

1 tbsp of canola oil

Few olives for decoration (optional)

Preparation:

Pour 3 cups of water in a pot. Bring it to boil and add macaroni and salt. Boil macaroni for about 3 minutes (rice flour macaroni take less time to cook). You can also use the package instructions to cook macaroni, if you're not sure. Remove from heat and drain.

In a bowl, combine tuna with homemade cashew cream. Mash well with a fork.

In a large saucepan, combine the olive oil with canola oil. Heat up over a medium temperature and add tuna mixture. Fry for about 15-20 minutes stirring occasionally. Add macaroni and mix well. Cover the saucepan and allow macaroni to heat up. Serve warm with some olives.

Nutrition information per serving: Kcal: 224, Protein: 33g, Carbs: 44.3g, Fats: 12g

17. Orange Barbecue Chicken

Ingredients:

2 pounds of chicken tighs

2 medium onions, chopped

2 small chili peppers

1 cup of chicken broth

¼ cup of fresh orange juice

1 tsp of orange extract

2 tbsp of olive oil

1 tsp of barbecue seasoning mix

1 small red onion, chopped

Preparation:

Heat up the olive oil in a large saucepan. Add chopped onions and fry for several minutes, over a medium temperature – until golden color.

Combine chili peppers, orange juice and orange extract. Mix well in a food processor for 20-30 seconds. Add this mixture into a saucepan and stir well. Reduce heat to simmer.

Coat the chicken with barbecue seasoning mix and put into a saucepan. Add chicken broth and bring it to a boil. Cook over a medium temperature until the water evaporates. Remove from the heat.

Preheat the oven to 350 degrees. Place the chicken into a large baking dish. Bake for about 15 minutes to get a nice crispy, golden brown color.

Nutrition information per serving: Kcal: 170 Protein: 38g, Carbs: 11g, Fats: 21g

18. Grilled Veal Steak with Vegetables

Ingredients:

1 pound of veal steak, about 1 inch thick

1 medium red pepper

1 medium green pepper

1 small onion

3 tbsp of olive oil

Salt and pepper to taste

Preparation:

Wash and pat dry the steak with a kitchen paper. Heat up the olive oil over a medium temperature and fry the meat for about 20 minutes (about 10 on each side). Remove from the heat and set aside.

Wash and cut vegetables into thin strips. Add some salt and pepper. Cook for about 15 minutes stirring constantly.

Serve immediately.

Nutrition information per serving: Calories: 309 Protein: 35g Carbohydrates: 7.1g Fats: 17g

19. Easy Chicken Stew

Ingredients:

1 pound of chicken thighs

3 cups of chicken broth

3 red onions, chopped

2 large carrots, chopped

2 medium-sized sweet potatoes

½ tsp of salt

¼ tsp of peper

Preparation:

Place the ingredients in a deep pot. Add chicken broth and season with salt and pepper.

Set the heat to minimum and cook for about two hours, or until the meat is done and vegetables soft.

Nutrition information per serving: Calories490 Protein: 62g Carbohydrates: 39g Fats: 23g

20. Pan Roasted Lamb with Rice

Ingredients:

2 pounds of lamb cutlets, boneless

1 cup of brown rice

2 ½ cup of water

1 tsp of ground turmeric

5 tbsp of olive oil

¼ cup of lemon juice

3 cloves of garlic, minced

½ tsp of sea salt

½ tsp of ground pepper

1 tbsp of rice flour

¼ cup of water

Preparation:

Boil 2 ½ cup of water and add rice. Cook over medium temperature for about 10 minutes, or until the water evaporates. Remove from the heat and add ground turmeric. This will give your rice a nice golden color but it will also add some amazing nutritional values to your food. Cover the rice and set aside.

Wash and pat dry the cutlets. Heat up the olive oil over a medium temperature. Add the cutlets into a skillet and cook for about 10 minutes on each side. Reduce the heat to low and add rice flour, minced garlic, lemon juice, salt, pepper and some more water (¼ cup should be enough). Stir well and cook for about 15 minutes.

Serve with rice.

Nutrition information per serving: Calories: 411 Protein: 45g Carbohydrates: 19g Fats: 21g

Dinner Recipes:

21. Marinated Salmon Slices

Ingredients:

2 pounds of fresh salmon, sliced into 1 inch slices

1 cup of extra virgin olive oil

3 tbsp of freshly squeezed lemon juice

1 tbsp of finely chopped rosemary

1 tsp of dry oregano, ground

1 dry bay leaf, crushed

1 tsp of salt

1 tbsp of cayenne pepper

Preparation:

Combine the olive oil with lemon juice, chopped rosemary, dry oregano, bay leaf, salt, and cayenne pepper. Stir well to combine.

Using a kitchen brush, spread this mixture over the salmon sliced. Let it stand for about 10-15 minutes.

Meanwhile, preheat the grill pan over a medium-high heat. Grill the salmon slices for 3 minutes, on each side.

Nutrition information per serving: Calories: 261 Protein: 26g Carbohydrates: 0g Fats: 16g

22. Citrus Sea Bream

Ingredients:

1 piece of fresh sea bream

1 cup of olive oil

½ lemon, sliced

¼ cup of freshly squeezed lemon juice

1 tsp of dry rosemary, ground

1 tbsp of fresh parsley, finely chopped

3 garlic cloves, crushed

¼ tsp of sea salt

Preparation:

Wash and clean the fish. Pat dry and cut in half.

Combine the olive oil, lemon juice, dry rosemary, fresh parsley, crushed garlic cloves, and sea salt in a large bowl. Soak the fish in this marinate and leave in the refrigerator for at least 30 minutes (it can stand in the refrigerator up to 2 hours).

Meanwhile, preheat the oven to 300 degrees. Spread some olive oil over a baking sheet and set aside.

Remove the fish from the refrigerator and transfer to a baking sheet. Add some of the marinade and cook for about 30 minutes.

Remove from the oven, sprinkle with some more marinade and serve with lemon slices and some vegetables of your choice.

Nutrition information per serving: Calories: 175 Protein: 31g Carbohydrates: 0.5g Fats: 21g

23. Vegetable Risotto

Ingredients:

1 cup of brown rice

1 medium-sized carrot, sliced

1 medium-sized zucchini, sliced

1 small tomato, roughly chopped

½ small eggplant, sliced

1 small red pepper, sliced

3 tbsp of extra virgin olive oil

½ tsp of salt

1 tsp of dry marjoram

Preparation:

Place the rice in a deep pot. Add 2 cups of water and bring it to a boil. Reduce the heat and cook until the water evaporates. Stir occasionally.

Heat up one tablespoon of olive oil over a medium-high heat. Add sliced carot and stir-fry for 3-4 minutes, stirring constantly. Combine with rice.

Stir in the remaining olive oil, zucchini, tomato, eggplant, red pepper, salt, and marjoram. Add one cup of water and continue to cook for another 10 minutes.

Nutrition information per serving: Calories: 220 Protein: 6g Carbohydrates: 51g Fats: 7.8g

24. Grilled Broccoli

Ingredients:

4oz fresh broccoli

Freshly ground black pepper to taste

Fresh parsley, chopped

3 tbsp of olive oil

Preparation:

Heat up the olive oil in a large grill pan. Place the broccoli and grill for 5-6 minutes, or until lightly charred.

Transfer to a plate and sprinkle with some pepper and parsley. Serve warm.

Serving tip:

Combine the chopped parsley with one garlic clove.

Nutrition information per 1 serving: Kcal: 40 Protein: 3.2g, Carbs: 7.5g, Fats: 3g

25. Grilled Trout

Ingredients:

7oz fresh trout steaks

¼ cup of chopped fresh coriander leaves

2 garlic cloves, minced

¼ cup of tablespoons of lemon juice

½ teaspoon smoked paprika

½ teaspoon cumin, ground

½ teaspoon chili powder

Ground black pepper to taste

Preparation:

Add the coriander, crushed garlic, paprika, cumin, chili powder, and lemon juice in a food processor and pulse to combine.

Transfer the mixture into a bowl, add the fish and gently toss to coat the fish evenly with sauce. Chill for at least 2 hours to allow the flavor to penetrate into the fish.

Remove the fish from the refrigerator and preheat the grill pan. Place the fish and grill for about 3 to 4 minutes on each side.

Remove the fish from the grill, transfer on a serving plate and serve with lemon or some vegetables of your choice.

Nutrition information per 1 serving: Kcal: 143 Protein: 21g, Carbs: 0g, Fats: 7g

26. Grilled zucchini

Ingredients:

4oz zucchini

¼ cup of fresh lemon juice

¼ tsp of sea salt

1 tsp dry rosemary

¼ tsp of freshly ground black pepper

Preparation:

Whisk together lemon juice, sea salt, rosemary, and black pepper. Wash and peel zucchini. Cut into thin slices. Brush each slice with this mixture.

Preheat a non-stick grill pan, or an electric grill, over a medium-high temperature. Grill the zucchini for several minutes on each side. Serve warm.

Nutrition information per 1 serving: Kcal: 18 Protein: 1.3g, Carbs: 3.8g, Fats: 0.2g

27. Grilled Shrimps

Ingredients:

2 lbsfresh large shrimps, whole

3 tbsp. extra-virgin olive oil

Sea salt to taste

Preparation:

Make sure you use the best, extra-virgin olive oil for to get a maximum flavor.

Heat up some olive oil in a grill pan, over a medium-high heat. Three tablespoons will be enough. Place the shrimps in it and grill for 5 minutes, turning to char all sides.

Remove from the heat and use some kitchen paper to soak up the excess oil.

Transfer to a plate and sprinkle with some salt. Serve immediately.

Nutrition information per serving: Kcal: 224, Protein: 27.1g, Carbs: 10g, Fats: 5g

<u>Add extra flavor:</u>

Extra virgin olive oil is definitely one of my favorite ingredients in food. Its tender flavor and a unique smell is not the only reason why this liquid gold is so popular. Olive oil is loaded with antioxidants and healthy fats. Its health benefits are something everybody agrees on. A drizzle of olive oil in this protein-packed meal will protect your heart and blood vessels. And to make things even more interesting, healthy garlic and chopped parsley topping will turn theseshrimps into a poetry of flavors.

In a small bowl, combine 1 cup of olive oil with 1 tbsp of finely chopped parsley, 2 crushed garlic cloves, 1 tsp of dry rosemary, ½ tsp of salt, ¼ tsp of pepper. Use to marinate the shrimps before grilling.

Drizzle two tablespoons of this marinade over grilled shrimps. Tastes perfect every time!

28. Stewed Spinach

Ingredients:

7oz fresh spinach

2 tbsp fresh coriander, finely chopped

1 tsp apple cider vinegar

3 tbsp extra virgin olive oil

Fresh water

Preparation:

Fill in a large saucepan with fresh water and bring to a boil. Wash the spinach and add to the saucepan. Cover and reduce the heat to minimum. Cook for about 2-3 minutes, until spinach has wilted.

Remove from the heat and drain. Allow it to cool for a while.

Transfer the spinach to a skillet. Add olive oil and stir-fry for several minutes, stirring constantly. Remove from the heat and season with fresh coriander and apple cider vinegar.

Nutrition information per serving: Kcal: 38, Protein: 3g, Carbs: 5g, Fats: 7g

29. Lettuce Wraps

Ingredients:

1 pound of salmon meat, minced

1 tablespoon mixed vegetable seasoning

¼ cup minced red onion

2 tablespoons bell pepper, minced

½ cup tomato puree

8 large Iceberg lettuce leaves

½ cup cashew cream

Olive oil

½ cup of water or chicken stock

Preparation:

Heat up some oil in a non-stick pan over medium-high temperature. Add the salmon meat and cook for 5 minutes, stirring constantly. Stir in the vegetable seasoning, onions, bell pepper and tomato puree and cook it for 5 minutes. Pour in the water or stock, cover with lid and bring it to a boil. Reduce the heat to low and simmer for about 20 minutes, or until the liquid has reduced in half. Remove the pan from heat and set it aside.

Prepare the lettuce leaves and place them on a work surface. Portion the meat into the 6 to 8 lettuce leaves. Add cashew cream and wrap.

Nutrition information per serving: Kcal: 249, Protein: 20.5g, Carbs: 7g, Fats: 16g

30. Grilled Tuna Steaks

Ingredients:

¼ cup of chopped fresh coriander leaves

3 garlic cloves, minced

2 tablespoons of lemon juice

½ cup olive oil

4 tuna steaks

½ teaspoon smoked paprika

½ teaspoon cumin, ground

½ teaspoon chili powder

Salt and black pepper

Preparation:

Add the coriander, garlic, paprika, cumin, chilli powder and lemon juice in a food processor and pulse to combine. Gradually add in the oil and mix the ingredients until a smooth mixture.

Transfer the mixture into a bowl, add the fish and gently toss to coat the fish evenly with sauce. Chill for at least 2 hours to allow the flavors to penetrate into the fish.

Remove the fish from the chiller and preheat the grill. Lightly brush the grid with oil, place the fish and grill for about 3 to 4 minutes on each side.

Remove the fish from the grill, transfer on a serving plate and serve with lemon wedges or some vegetables

Nutrition information per serving: Kcal: 110, Protein: 25g, Carbs: 0g, Fats: 4g

Salad Recipes

31. Cucumber Salad

Ingredients:

3.5 oz cucumber, peeled and sliced

1 tbsp of fresh lime juice

3 tbsp of extra virgin olive oil

2 tbsp of finely chopped parsley

2 garlic cloves

½ tsp of salt

¼ tsp of freshly ground black pepper

Preparation:

Peel and slice the cucumber. Transfer to a serving platter. Combine the olive oil with fresh lime juice, chopped parsley, crushed garlic cloves, salt, and pepper. Stir well to combine. Pour the mixture over cucumber and let it stand in the refrigerator for about one hour before serving.

Nutrition information per serving: Kcal: 121, Protein: 2g, Carbs: 3g, Fats: 13g

32. Rice Salad

Ingredients:

1 cup of long grain, brown rice

3 spring onions, finely chopped

½ cup of sweet corn

1 medium-sized red bell pepper

A handful of chopped mint

2 tbsp of extra virgin olive oil

1 tbsp of apple cider vinegar

Salt to taste

Preparation:

Place the rice in a deep pot. Add 3 cups of water and bring it to a boil. Reduce the heat, cover and simmer until the water evaporates. Remove from the heat and cool.

Combine the ingredients in a deep bowl. Add olive oil, apple cider vinegar, and some salt to taste. Toss well to combine.

Serve cold.

Nutrition information per serving: Kcal: 395 Protein: 2g, Carbs: 38g, Fats: 18g

33. Fresh Vegetable Salad

Ingredients:

3.5oz lettuce, roughly chopped

1 onion, peeled and sliced

1 medium-sized tomato, chopped

A handful of soy beans, soaked

3 tbsp of extra virgin olive oil

1 tbsp of apple cider vinegar

1 tsp of fresh rosemary, finely chopped

¼ tsp of salt

Preparation:

In a small bowl combine the olive oil with apple cider vinegar, rosemary, and salt. Mix well to combine.

Place the vegetables in a large bowl. Add soaked soy beans and drizzle with marinade.

Serve cold.

Nutrition information per serving: Kcal: 145 Protein: 19g, Carbs: 14g, Fats: 11g

34. Sweet Carrot Salad

Ingredients:

1 medium-sized carrot, sliced

2oz baby spinach

1 medium-sized tomato, finely chopped

2oz rice spaghetti, soaked

1 small tomato, finely chopped

¼ cup of fresh blueberries

For the dressing:

¼ cup of honey

¼ cup of fresh lime juice

1 tsp of dijon mustard

¼ tbsp of ground cumin

Preparation:

Soak the rice spaghetti in water for about 15 minutes. Drain and transfer to a bowl.

Add chopped spinach, tomato, sliced carrot, and blueberries. Toss to combine.

In another bowl, combine the marinade ingredients and mix well. Drizzle over salad.

Serve.

Nutrition information per serving: Kcal: 98 Protein: 4.5g, Carbs: 19g, Fats: 6g

35. Spring Salad with Black Olives

Ingredients:

5 cherry tomatoes, whole

A handful of black olives

1 medium-sized onion, peeled and sliced

2 radishes, sliced

A handful of lamb's lettuce

2 tbsp of freshly squeezed lime juice

3 tbsp of extra virgin olive oil

Salt to taste

Preparation:

Place the vegetables in a large bowl. Add olive oil, fresh lime juice and some salt to taste. Toss to combine.

Nutrition information per serving: Kcal: 41 Protein: 1g, Carbs: 7g, Fats: 4g

36. Green Bean Salad

Ingredients:

1 pound green beans

¼ cup of extra virgin olive oil

2 garlic cloves, crushed

1 tbsp of lime juice

Preparation:

Boil a pot of water and add one teaspoon of salt and green beans. Cook until tender. Rinse and drain.

Meanwhile, combine the crushed garlic with olive oil and lime juice. Pour over beans and serve.

Nutrition information per serving: Kcal: 138 Protein: 5g, Carbs: 18g, Fats: 6.7g

37. Raspberry Salad

Ingredients:

A handful of lettuce, torn

1 tbsp of pumpkin seeds

1 cup of fresh raspberries

1 tbsp of fresh rosemary, chopped

2 tbsp of fresh lime juice

1 tsp of cumin

1 tsp of agave syrup

Preparation:

Combine the lettuce with pumpkin seeds and raspberries in a bowl. In a separate bowl, combine the agave syrup with lime juice, cumin, and fresh rosemary. Drizzle over salad and serve.

Nutrition information per serving: Kcal: 29 Protein: 4g, Carbs: 10g, Fats: 3g

38. Cherry Tomatoes with Broccoli

Ingredients

2 cups of broccoli, cut in half

2 large tomatoes, chopped roughly

2 tbsp of olive oil

1 tbsp of dry salad seasoning of your choice (I use dry parsley)

salt to taste

3 cups of water

Preparation:

Bring the water to boil in a deep pot. Add broccoli and cook for about 20 minutes, or until soft. You can try this with a fork. Remove from the heat and drain. Allow it to cool for a while and cut each broccoli in half. Wash and roughly chop the tomatoes. Combine it with broccoli in a bowl and season with olive oil and salad seasoning.

You can add a few garlic cloves, but this is optional.

Nutrition information per serving: Kcal: 88 Protein: 7g, Carbs: 31g, Fats: 12g

39. Seafood Salad

Ingredients:

1 small pack of frozen mixed seafood

1 tbsp of olive oil

1 small onion

1 cup of cherry tomatoes

1 tsp of chopped, dry rosemary

1 tbsp of sweet corn

¼ tsp of salt

1 tbsp of freshly squeezed lemon juice

Preparation

Heat up the olive oil in a saucepan. Fry frozen seafood for about 15 minutes, over a medium temperature (try the octopus, it takes the most time to tender). You can add some water if necessary – about ¼ of cup will be enough. Stir occasionally. Remove from frying pan and allow it to cool for about an hour.

Meanwhile, chop the vegetables into very small pieces. In a large bowl, combine the vegetables with corn, seafood and season with salt, rosemary and lemon juice.

Nutrition information per serving: Kcal: 315 Protein: 27g, Carbs: 15g, Fats: 12g

40. Dandelion Greens Salad

Ingredients:

2oz fresh dandelion greens, roughly chopped

1oz tomato, finely chopped

½ cup of fresh lemon juice

1 tbsp of mustard

Sea salt to taste

Preparation:

Roughly chop the dandelion greens and place in a bowl. Pour the lemon juice over it and let it stand for about 30 minutes. Remove from the bowl and drain. Add finely chopped tomato and mustard. Season with salt and one teaspoon of apple cider vinegar. Serve immediately.

Nutrition information per serving: Kcal: 31 Protein: 2.3g, Carbs: 7.1g, Fats: 0.5g

Snack Recipes

41. Green Bean Puree

Ingredients:

4oz fresh green beans

Spices of your choice

Preparation:

Clean the beans and place in a pot. Add enough water and cook until tender. Remove from the heat and rinse well under the cold water. Place in a food processor and mix until smooth mixture. Season with some spices of your choice and serve warm.

Nutrition information per serving: Kcal: 35 Protein: 2.5g, Carbs: 8g, Fats: 0.3g

42. Broccoli Soup

Ingredients:

2oz fresh broccoli

A handful of fresh parsley, finely chopped

1 tsp of dry thyme

1 tbsp of fresh lemon juice

¼ tsp of ground chili pepper

Preparation:

Place the broccoli in a deep pot and pour enough water to cover. Bring it to a boil and cook until tender. Remove from the heat and drain. Transfer to a food processor. Add fresh parsley, thyme, and about ½ cup of water. Pulse until smooth mixture. Return to a pot and add some more water. Bring it to a boil and cook for several minutes, over a minimum temperature. Sprinkle with ground chili pepper and add fresh lemon juice. Serve warm.

Nutrition information per serving: Kcal: 19 Protein: 1.6g, Carbs: 3.7g, Fats: 0.2g

43. Mashed broccoli with Mint

Ingredients:

8oz broccoli, chopped

1 cup of coconut milk

1 tbsp of vanilla extract

1 tsp of dry mint (or any other seasoning of your choice)

Preparation:

Place the broccoli in a deep pot. Add enough water to cover. Bring it to a boil and cook for 15-20 minutes, or until soft. When done, drain and drain and transfer to a food processor. Add dry mint, coconut milk, and vanilla extract. Pulse to combine. If the mixture is too thick, you can add some more coconut milk.

Nutrition information per serving: Kcal: 32 Protein: 17g, Carbs: 8g, Fats: 5g

44. Cauliflower Soup

Ingredients:

2oz cauliflower (must be weighed raw)

1 tsp of fresh mint, finely chopped

¼ tsp of dry coriander, crushed

Pepper to taste

Fresh water

Preparation:

Place the cauliflower and dry coriander into a deep pot. Add enough water to cover and bring it to a boil. Cook for about 10-15 minutes. Remove from the heat.

Blend the soup with stick blender. Add some pepper to taste and garnish with fresh mint. Serve warm.

Nutrition information per serving: Kcal: 17 Protein: 2g, Carbs: 4g, Fats: 1g

ADDITIONAL TITLES FROM THIS AUTHOR

70 Effective Meal Recipes to Prevent and Solve Being Overweight: Burn Fat Fast by Using Proper Dieting and Smart Nutrition

By

Joe Correa CSN

48 Acne Solving Meal Recipes: The Fast and Natural Path to Fixing Your Acne Problems in Less Than 10 Days!

By

Joe Correa CSN

41 Alzheimer's Preventing Meal Recipes: Reduce or Eliminate Your Alzheimer's Condition in 30 Days or Less!

By

Joe Correa CSN

70 Effective Breast Cancer Meal Recipes: Prevent and Fight Breast Cancer with Smart Nutrition and Powerful Foods

By

Joe Correa CSN